smart Casual

AND OTHER EXPRESSIONS I HATE

smart Casual

AND OTHER EXPRESSIONS I HATE

JEREMY TAYLOR

Andean Publishing

New York

Copyright © 2020 by Jeremy Taylor
All rights reserved. Names, characters, places, and incidents may be the product of the author's imagination or are used fictitiously or have been changed, and any resemblance to actual persons, living or dead, businesses, companies, events, or locales is entirely coincidental.

Andean Publishing
1420 York Avenue
New York, NY 10021

No parts of this book may be reproduced, scanned, or distributed in any printed or electronic form without permission. Please do not participate in or encourage piracy of copyrighted materials in violation of the author's rights.

Images in this book are from www.pixabay.com and are released under Pixabay License.

Taylor, Jeremy // Smart Casual
Jeremy, Taylor // Andean Publishing

Library of Congress Control Number: 2020921164
ISBN 9781736127711 (ebook) I ISBN 9781736127704 (hardcover)

Purchase only authorized editions.

Contents

Random 1
Entertainment 29
Animals 39
Forest 55
Sports 63
Food 77
Violence and Weapons 89
Body Parts 101
Numbers 115
Money and Names 133
Travel 143

FOR ANDRES,

THE ONLY PERSON WHO CAN PUT UP WITH MY SHIT.

Smart casual is an ambiguously defined Western dress code that is generally considered casual wear but with smart (in a sense of "well dressed") components of a proper lounge suit from traditional informal wear.

–WIKIPEDIA

I chose this title because it makes you think, right?

–JEREMY TAYLOR

I do not like to think at all.

–KANYE WEST (HARPER'S BAZAAR, JULY 2016)

Part One

Random

WET BLANKET

When somebody calls you a wet blanket, they're fat-shaming you. Why? Have you ever tried moving a wet blanket from the washer to the dryer? It weighs a bushel and a Chris Christie.

A wet blanket, aside from weighing a gigaton, is also someone who spoils the fun. When was the last time a blanket, a sheet, or a pillow ruined your party? If you simply need a reason to complain about anything, you're not a wet blanket. Instead you're 90, live in Florida, and your mucus is out of control.

BEGGARS CAN'T BE CHOOSERS

First of all, why the fuck not? You're telling me—in all seriousness—that when I beg on the street (minding my own business) and some asshole offers me a tuna sandwich, I can't say, "Fuck you, motherfucker! I'm a vegetarian!"?

Don't tell me what to do! It infringes on my rights as an American and as a Democrat. Just because I'm in a dire situation, it doesn't mean I'll become a ruthless animal and eat tuna from a can. I have standards and I won't go for less.

I'm not Melania Trump.

PS. If you like to bend over like in the picture, you're not begging—you're getting pegged.

"Yo, have a buck?"

"Um, I'm a dog."

"So? What's your point?"

BETTER LATE THAN NEVER

Most Hollywood actors think they can start their careers at 41 like Melissa McCarthy on *Bridesmaids*, but she's an exception. If I see you on TV and you're 41, you better be dead for 14 years like Amy Winehouse, pop pills like Paula Abdul, or have a Greek accent like Lindsay Lohan. To sum it up: be fucked up way before you're 41.

BTW, I love *Bridesmaids*! Do you remember the scene when Kristen Wiig makes cupcakes, and there are close-ups of her hands? Turns out, those hands belonged to a stand-in (when Wiig was busy filming other scenes). The same happened in *Jurassic World*. When Katie McGrath couldn't film, they just put a dinosaur in her place.

CALL IT A DAY

When something is done, you call it a day. I asked Kendra Wilkinson to name one state a week ago and she's still working on it—so she clearly doesn't know what "call it a day" means. The only thing she knows how to finish in one day is *Mean Girls*.

OFF THE RECORD

What record? What are you even talking about? Are you telling me the rest of our conversation was recorded? It was a stupid conversation to begin with!

"How was your date?"

"He was handsome, but—off the record—he was four inches long and had bad breath. We made out for hours anyway."

Four inches and halitosis—for hours? Off the record, that should go *on* the record. Are you self-punishing yourself somehow?

Besides, if I wanted to record anything, I'd record myself on video and do what Kim Kardashian did: I'd insert a VHS tape into my camcorder (yes, I'm old), hit "RECORD" and let the housekeeper (my mom) discover it "by mistake."

TELL ME ABOUT IT

This expression gives people an excuse to not listen. When I tell a story and hear "Tell me about it," it makes me wanna stab someone. Why aren't you fucking listening? Unless you're deaf or dead, there are no excuses. (Off the record, I may have murdered someone when I heard, "Tell me about it." My bad.)

MY BAD

You bump into me from behind as I'm trying to shoplift extra virgin olive oil (it's so expensive) and you say, "Oops, my bad."

Yeah, no shit. Anything else you'd like to add, bitch? Perhaps something about your parents wanting an abortion, but they couldn't do it because it was in Missouri? Oh, sorry, my bad. I meant misery.

WHITE LIE

I hate this racist expression because it only works if you're white and if you lie. I weigh one hundred and fifty pounds. See? A white lie.

WHAT'S NOT TO LIKE?

Are you sure? Now stand in front of the mirror and ask that again, Lyle Lovett.

Do it again, but turn on the lights this time.

KEEPER

You know who a keeper is? Paul Sheldon in *Misery* because Kathy Bates kept him.

Speaking of *Misery*, I loathe that film. I couldn't sleep for five days after watching it, thinking about a person I was holding captive.

So I let him go.

I said, "Michael, I know we've been together for five months but I feel bad."

He said, "What do you mean?"

I said, "We're breaking up—that's what I mean!"

"But why?"

"Blame Kathy fucking Bates!"

IT'S NOT ROCKET SCIENCE

Calm down, I know. All Lindsay Lohan asked was, "What's one plus one?" Jeez. Be patient with her. Not all of us graduated first grade.

TOP-NOTCH

A notch is a deep, narrow mountain pass. You start hiking in your Walmart boots, all the way to the top of the mountain and you what? You think that you're alone in the woods? With your thoughts? You'll understand the meaning of life? No. There's now a fucking bear running after you.

SMART CASUAL

What's wrong with the "stupid formal" I'm wearing? I have a job interview with Jessica Simpson.

This expression—smart casual—hurts people's feelings. I heard Roger Stone in Edgecombe Correctional Facility has only two outfits to pick from: *Orange Clever* or *Orange-You-Glad-You're-Not-at-Rikers-Fish?* and neither outfit goes with his skin tone. Roger is also upset about being called a fish, but why not? He resembles a fucking whale.[1]

[1] A fish is a new inmate in men's prison. I never liked the term "fish." If you want to insult a gay man, call him Marilyn Manson. Or, if he's straight, call him Marilyn Monroe.

THE JURY IS STILL OUT

Out where? Drinking? There's nothing I loathe more than when people are drinking without me!

Once, I served on a jury for twenty-five days and I was the foreman. The judge saw me and said, "This is the first for us, a *fore*man with *fore*skin."

I said, "Is that what impresses you, Your Honor? *For*give me *for fore*shadowing, but the man sitting be*fore* us is not guilty because he has an alibi. The *fore*nsic analysis will indicate that on the day of the murder he and I fucked *for four* hours, and I still have his sperm in my *fore*gut."

LOSE ONE'S MARBLES

How is that an expression expressing erratic behavior? Do people know what a marble even is? It's a toy! A spherical object! Yes, like the sun. How could you lose the sun? Are you dumb, or is your name Busy Philipps (who is drop-dead gorgeous, by the way)? But what kind of a name is Busy? That's plagiarism!

That's what Octomom named her pussy.

DROP-DEAD GORGEOUS

Why is it appropriate to say that someone is drop-dead gorgeous when you hang out in Central Park but inappropriate at the morgue? I hate double standards![1] Yes, she dropped dead, but she's still gorgeous. Even the mortician fucked her.

[1] I find it unfair that "double standards" has a negative meaning. So, like . . . Let's say I have standards, okay?—PLAY PRETEND WITH ME—And this is my perfect match: 25, rich, 5'8''. Then I double my standards, so now he's: 50, filthy rich, 11'6'' and named Dick Van Dyke.[2]

Similarly, Mariah Carey took her boobs and doubled them. What's the big fucking deal?

[2] Dyke and Dick in the same sentence? How is that even possible?[3]

[3] My lesbian friend said the lesbians prefer the word "butch," or in Ellen DeGeneres' case, "swashbuckler."[4]

[4] I don't have any lesbian friends. That was smoke and mirrors. Haw haw.

SMOKE AND MIRRORS

I actually love this expression because I love mirrors. I especially love having sex in front of them. How else do you think I've learned all my angles? Not through fucking trigonometry, I'll tell you that.

When it comes to smoke, however, it depends. If my kitchen gets smoky, I don't like it. Mainly because I probably burned my pot brownies and I hate when my brownies are too brown. If the smoke is spewing from a building nearby—that's totally fine; my neighbor Carole Baskin is dumb as a doornail and burns everything. Mostly her former husbands.

DUMB AS A DOORNAIL

First of all, is it "dumb as a doornail" or "dumb as a doorman"? I've heard both. In either case, the expression makes no sense. A doornail is a stud set in a door for strength. How can a doornail be dumb? Does it have JWoww's brain? If everything set inside something is "dumb," then I guess that explains those people inside my TV on Fox News.

GRAVITY OF THE SITUATION

Ugh, I hate gravity. It pulls all body parts down, including the skin—and my saggy face needs a fucking facelift!

LEARNING CURVE

Why is it called a "curve"? When I was in college, we studied the material from something called a book, and books are rectangular—not curvy. The only thing that's curvy in college (aside from curvy girls and curvy paths from sexual escapades) is the Curve cologne.

UNDER

THE WEATHER

Why is "under the weather" an expression for "not feeling well"? What does it have to do with "the weather" or being "under"? Just because a hurricane hit and knocked your house upside down, that doesn't mean you're automatically unwell. Trust me, there's always a reason to celebrate. Just think of the insurance policy payout! And it was hurricane Maria, the same name as your wife. Maybe it's telling you it's time for a divorce? Just saying.

Part Two

Entertainment

NO DICE

"No dice" means "an unfavorable result." Huh, interesting. I thought an unfordable result was the movie *Cats*.

BREAK A LEG

My ex-boyfriend was an actor, and he made me say this phrase repeatedly at every performance. I never understood why, so one time I brought my voodoo doll and wished he broke his leg. He did. I really don't understand why he was such a masochist. Would you say he ate his words?

PS. Did you know that "break a leg" is a dead metaphor, which is a figure of speech that has lost its meaning due to too much usage? For a second I thought I was talking about Kellyanne Conway's mouth, which lost its meaning due to too much usage. Have you heard her filibusters? The bitch would say stupid shit but would never answer important questions.

One time at an interview, I asked her why she has two names, Kelly and Anne—which is so narcissistic—and Conway said, "Get your act together. I have three names: Kelly, Anne, and Elizabeth."

I asked, "Is that because you're from Atco, NJ, which has a population of five and you're three of them? Acting as the mayor, the counselor, and the town's own whore?"

She declined to answer. Typical Kellyanne Conway.

GET YOUR ACT TOGETHER

I hate it when I get trashed and start kissing everyone, someone at a party will always say, "Get your act together!"

Who's acting? Jeez. I'm horny and I *do* wanna kiss everyone.

Don't worry, guys, I'm not a perv, and I only have two outstanding arrest warrants. Like, you don't have to be scared of me. They're OUTSTANDING warrants— so they're FABULOUS.

PS. "Get your act together" means "to organize yourself so that you do things effectively." So for a mass shooter, the first thing you do is register as a white supremacist, buy a gun, and join QAnon forums.

PS. This is not a mass shooter. This is a pig. I know. While not all white supremacists look like mass shooters, all mass shooters look like pigs.

FACE THE MUSIC

Do what now? Last time I checked my *ears* were responsible for listening to music, not my face. Am I wrong? My face is for fillers and Botox, not music.

Music is nothing but sound waves, and if I really want some waves on my face, I'll grab a surfboard and hit the Pacific Ocean.

By the way, the Pacific Ocean is anything but passive; it's aggressive. Kind of like Harvey Weinstein's roommate at Wende Correctional Facility.

Speaking of conservative assholes, in the book by Laura Anne Ingraham—*Shut Up & Sing*—there's more white space than white people in her dumb life. If you read her book, you'll need sunglasses, or you'll get snow-blinded.

Look, bitch, if you wanna insert white space all over the fucking place, at least insert some fun pictures as well—like in this coloring book. I'm selflessly helping American businesses to sell more crayons and markers so they could make a buck. And what do you do instead, Laura Anne Ingraham? You call gay people sodomites. But have you checked your fucking pubes? There are ACTUAL mites there.

Part Three

Animals

PUT LIPSTICK ON A PIG

It means to "make superficial changes to something in a fruitless attempt to make it better."

Ugh, I don't wanna mention Carole Baskin, but I will. We know her tricky nature, right? When she buried her husband, a tree grew in his place, which I personally believe is good for the environment. But you know what happened to the rubber gloves? A rubber fig grew in their place. Carole—without missing a beat—put lipstick on a pig by planting chrysanthemums in its place to hide the evidence. Chrysanthemums are inappropriate in the spring! But they covered any lingering smell.

MAKE AN ELEPHANT
OUT OF A FLY

That means to overreact. Oh, FUCKING REALLY? WHO'S OVERREACTING? Elephants are almost extinct so we must do everything in our power to preserve them. So I made elephant preserves. Yum!

STOOL PIGEON

A stool pigeon is a person acting as a decoy, but a stall pigeon? It's a yoga pose but one performs it in a bathroom stall. I don't get why anyone would do yoga in a stall, much like I don't get Goya's CEO endorsing Donald Trump, and much like I don't get cow farts—which release up to 85 gallons of methane per day. What the fuck do they eat? Black Goya beans?

COLD TURKEY

I hate that Kim Kardashian quit her acting career in porn cold turkey. Who knows what would have happened? I foresee something insane. Like, you google "Kim," but instead of pictures of Kim Jong-Un, communism, and nuclear bombs, you get a link for nipple clamps. So much classier.

Here's a fun, keto, and low-calorie recipe for a cold turkey sandwich: you'll need two white buns, cold turkey, and mayo. So you take Ivanka Trump's butt cheeks, stuff cold turkey between them, and if you're out of mayo, don't worry. Something or someone white will always be around her.

HAPPY AS
A CLAM

Have you ever seen a clam? It looks, feels, and smells like a vagina, but, at least in Lisa Rinna's case, you could probably find a pearl or a diamond inside. Just a guess on my part. I mean, a vagina is a warm, dark place, just a perfect climate for growing pearls. I'd grow a Dracaena in mine; they're picky about their environment too.

THE BIRDS AND THE BEES

Lady Gaga refers to her fans as the "Little Monsters," Carole Baskin refers to her fans and her dead husbands (I'm pretty sure it's plural) as cool "Cats and Kittens," but the company Goya after endorsing Donald Trump? They call their customers the "Birds and the Bees." Why? Your guess is as good as mine. Well, the bees are disappearing—that's one—and the birds are their only customers at this point. Oh, right, and the cows, so they could fart after eating their black beans.

WILD GOOSE CHASE

Who fucking chases wild geese? Have you ever tried a baked goose breast? Even with a good sauce it's oily and rubbery, and if I wanted oily and rubbery I'd swallow a lubricated condom.

PS. Do you agree that Melania Trump resembles a goose?

Roasted goose recipe:

Preheat your oven to 350 degrees Fahrenheit and put in a frozen pizza for eight minutes. In the meantime, watch Melania Trump being roasted for doing something stupid again, like remodeling the White House Rose Garden.

Do you know where that goose Melania Trump came from? Slovenia. What do Slovenians know about fucking roses? Well, you'll be happy to know that Melania Trump thought the Rose Garden was a garden full of one-hundred-dollar bills. She's street, after all, and only speaks slang. Anyone could make a stupid mistake like that, right? Just like she's been trying to send an SOS text to get rescued from the White House but keeps sending LOL or #LOL by mistake.

BIG FISH IN A SMALL POND

Don't stick big animals into small cages. "Big fish in a small pond" is pure animal abuse, and I'm all about freedom!

The Petition:

"Free big cats, you dumb bitch, Carole Baskin! Free Willy from the amusement park, Rae Lindsley. And free most inmates from prisons, Mister President—especially those who are serving time for minor offenses (like smoking dope).

Keep Harvey Weinstein locked up, though."

—Thanks, the American people.

BEE'S KNEES

Does that expression refer to Beyoncé's knees? If your foot fetish involves knees, you must salivate excessively for such long licks. But wouldn't that take a long time as well? I'm a millennial, after all. If you have a fetish, fine, but you have one minute free—so use it wisely.

"What are you *doing*, Robert? I invited you for sex! Why are you going through my collection of lollipops? Now you have one minute and twenty seconds left. If you need to suck on something, pick a toe, any toe."

FOR THE BIRDS

"For the birds" means "insignificant." Cool beans. I guess we're still talking about Goya.

Part Four

Forest

WHOOPS-A-DAISY

Did you know that supermassive black holes swallow everything in sight, including stars, snow, and semen? Almost as much as Snooki. *Snort, snort, snort,* no more snow! Whoops-a-daisy!

Now that I have your attention . . . We have an overpopulation problem, people. If we don't send a black hole or Snooki to China or India to combat overpopulation by swallowing semen, we're barking up the wrong tree!

I'm aware it's a sunflower, and not a daisy.

Gimme a fucking break, people!

BARKING UP THE WRONG TREE

I hate this expression because of Snooki. Go swallow semen! Jeez. We're getting low on food in the world and I'm hungry.

I find it disturbing that some people bark, especially when trees are concerned. I heard two negatives make a positive, so if you're stupid, talk to someone stupid. If you need Sarah Huckabee Sanders' number, I have it:

1-800-DODO

A ROSE IS A ROSE IS A ROSE

No shit, Sherlock? A rose is a rose is a rose?

Leo Panzirer once visited his ex-wife—Leona Helmsley (the Queen of Mean)—at Rikers Correctional Facility, and she kept on chanting behind Plexiglass, "I'll kill you for breaking up with me, I'll kill you for breaking up with me, I'll kill you for breaking up with me."

Good Lord. I guess it's good he broke up with her—when he broke up with her—when he broke up with her.

PS. He broke up with her because Leona had a weird-looking rosebud on her butthole. So I guess not all roses are roses are roses. Hers were hemorrhoids were hemorrhoids were hemorrhoids.

BEAT AROUND THE BUSH

I hate violence, which is why if there's an expression about punching someone in the pubic area, I will loathe it. Especially if it's a thick, bushy one. I once lost a boot when I kicked my ex in his bush. They were UGGs and cost me an arm and a leg!

What's the difference between a sloth and a sleuth? Two fucking letters, that's what!

PS. "Beat around the bush" also refers to the Bush Administration, and if you beat off when any of the Bushes are present, you beat around the bush. Now, I'm not suggesting anything because masturbation is a sin, as any conservative would tell you. They'll also tell you that ALL LIVES MATTER. Nice, no? And they'll also tell you that guns don't kill people. (Not the "guns" on your arms as in "biceps," though, because the conservatives don't have those. They don't have time to work out as they're too busy defending the second amendment, hating the gays, and preventing immigrants from entering our lands by putting them in cages.)

Nice, no?

Okay, I'll stop beating around the bush and tell you nice and clear:

VOTE DEMOCRAT!

Part Five

Sports

SECOND BASE

I hate it when people compare their dating to baseball. The first base is when you French kiss, the second base is when you touch each other's hairy nipples (or in Anne Hathaway's case, her hairy camel toe), the third is when you move in, and the fourth is when you finally have intercourse and a joint Netflix account—or what the lesbians call the first date.

BALLPARK

Everything is about baseball in the United States—bats, second bases, and ballparks. When a proctologist asked Rock Hudson, "How many people have you slept with? What's the ballpark?" Rock showed the proctologist his anus and the doctor said, "Ah. An actual ballpark."

By the way, in gay lingo, Rock Hudson would most likely be a "top" or the person who does the "schtupping," which means his eggplant would enter another man's tuchus. So if there was a ballpark anywhere, it was in Lee Garlington's tuchus.

Lee Garlington is a blonde cutie-patootie, who in a 2018 interview said he'd had a relationship with Rock Hudson in the '60s. I'm jealous.

I wish Rock Hudson was a star now. Unfortunately, his name probably wouldn't be Rock Hudson because Rock wouldn't be in the closet and wouldn't need to hide his gay identity.

I heard he wanted to be named Kilo Gaye, Ken Biceps, or Klint Assmaster.

NOT A BIG FAN

Here is another expression I loathe because it originated with Carole Baskin. When the stench had become unbearable (you know what I mean, right?), she went to Target and asked if they had fans.

The associate asked, "Do you want a big fan?"

Carole said, "He was only five feet tall and his body doesn't smell *that* bad. So, please, not a big fan, my cool kitten."

KNOCK ON WOOD

I need more details. What kind of wood are we talking about? Birch, morning, Tiger Woods' wood? The last time Lea Michelle knocked on wood, she was drunk-knocking on her ex-boyfriend's wooden door, his roommate called the police, and she ended up with a restraining order (or that may have been wishful thinking on my part).

How is that an expression to wish someone good luck? If you're knocking on wood, you better be in a forest, and Chris Hemsworth's dick better be involved.

MONDAY MORNING QUARTERBACK

It's someone who passes judgments or criticizes something after an event. So when you (having never worked out a day in your life) criticize your aunt's Thanksgiving turkey the following day, suddenly you're a quarterback? Ripped and handsome? Quarterbacks are members of the offensive team, but I think calling yourself a quarterback is offensive. The only ball you ever played with was in your boxers, and your boxers, not you, were ripped.

Do me a favor and tell your cunty aunty her turkey is abysmal on the same day. I believe we'd live in a better world if we told the truth, right, Bernie Madoff? How's the correctional facility? I heard their turkey is so dry (like California) that it also became a fire hazard. Just the other day, when Bernie Madoff bent over to suck on some turkey, the whole facility burst into flames.

The following is not a funny story but you'll giggle: in 2012, a fire at the National Penitentiary in Comayagua, Honduras, killed 361 inmates. An investigation determined that the cause of the fire was an open flame that "accidentally" ignited combustible materials. Was it Tara Reid's whiskey breath? How do you *accidentally* burst into flames? Once an arsonist, always an arsonist—even in prison.

For example, John "Pillow Pyro" Orr set 2,000 fires before he got caught—that's dedication. Ironically, he was a firefighter, which is why he knew where the fires would start. He's serving life and 20 years, which is the most ridiculous thing. Once he dies in prison, are they gonna keep him there for another 20 years before they bury him? Was the jury a bunch of necrophiles?

The worst part of the story is that John "Pillow Pyro" Orr was caught because he wrote a book about a firefighter who was an arsonist. Bitch, you DON'T just do that. If you commit a crime, keep it to yourself. Humble-fucking-brag.

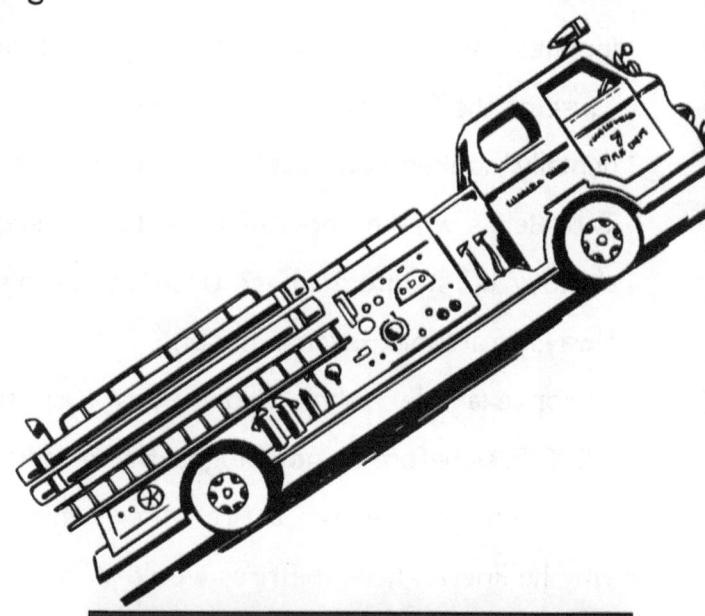

PS. Where the fuck are they're going uphill? To rescue a cat? Can someone tell them that Carole Baskin already snatched it? Thanks!

NOSEBLEED SECTION

This condescending expression means you can't afford better tickets, so you must sit all the way up on row 2,980. There's nothing above you but the pigeons with diarrhea. If that's not enough, now your nose starts bleeding. Like, who are you, a hemophilic? If you go up a few floors and your nose starts bleeding, you're not at a baseball game. You picked your nose too hard.

KEEP THE BALL ROLLING

Have you ever seen a football? You can't roll it because it's not round. It's shaped like Stewie Griffin's head on *The Family Guy*—a prolate spheroid—which is shaped after an inflated pig's bladder. Do you know why? That's what people used when football originated . . . Listen, if you need animal organs to play a game, don't call yourself a ballplayer. Call yourself a butcher.

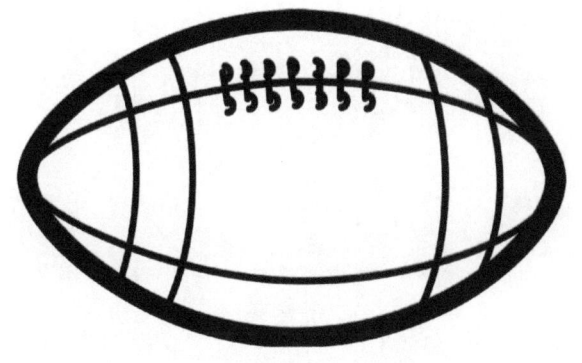

Part Six

Food

EAT ONE'S WORDS

Have you seen Charles Manson lately? He's gained a lot of weight while away on vacation (aka, a state prison in Corcoran, California). Of all places, you moron! If you need a vacation, go to Italy or France. Europe is so much classier. Have you what, never heard of the French paradox when they eat all they want, gain no weight, and live to a hundred?

Anyhow, my point is the food at the state prison is fattening. In fact, it's what they feed cows to make them bulk up fast for slaughtering. There's so much food Charles Manson can't possibly eat any more, so he eats words. He says a word, runs after it, and eats it. Wouldn't it be better, Charlie, if you didn't set up that sectarian group in the '60s? Now eat your words.

SPILL THE BEANS

Nobody is picking up your beans after you spilled them. You want me to bend over? Say so!

PIECE OF CAKE

I'm on a diet. Can you please stop bringing up food? When something is "easy," don't call it "a piece of cake." Call it after my mom. Listen, if my mom wasn't "easy" I wouldn't have ended up with twelve siblings. You know how much money I spend on Christmas?

Yo, whoever (whomever?) thought this picture resembled a cake, you're stupid. There's a roll of toilet paper for one; then I see two titties and Ivanka Trump's ear on the right . . .

DON'T CRY OVER SPILLED MILK

Oh, but you will. Listen up, bitch. When I invite you to my party, you better not spill anything on my white couch, white rugs, or my tighty-whities. Bleach is expensive. Right, Carole Baskin?

PS. I hate that Carole is the butt of every joke and the sole reason they're out of hatchets and shovels at my local Walmart. I'm trying to lose weight and make money, so I wanted to work as a gravedigger for a few months. On the black market, you could sell Michael Jackson's skeleton for $50,000, but now there are no shovels. Carole Baskin, if you're reading this, help the brother out and send me a shovel.

KNOW ONE'S ONIONS

When you're knowledgeable on a topic, you know your onions. Cool. Fair. But why can't you just at least brush your teeth? That onion breath is killing me.

TAKE THE WORDS OUT OF SOMEONE'S MOUTH

I hate people these days. The economy is so bad they'll steal just about anything, even the words out of my mouth. Where are you going to pawn them and make a profit? If you need to steal something, invest in a shovel and go tomb-raiding. Sure, it's scary, especially at night, but why are you scared of ghosts, anyway? They're white and friendly. Most of them are WASPs.

I hate ghosts because I hate "ghosting," a dating trend when someone talks to you and then disappears as if they've been "ghosts" all along.

Listen, if you've ever "ghosted" anyone, you're an asshole. Why? Because there's only one day a year when you can be a ghost and that's for Halloween, so why are "ghosting" all year long? So rude.

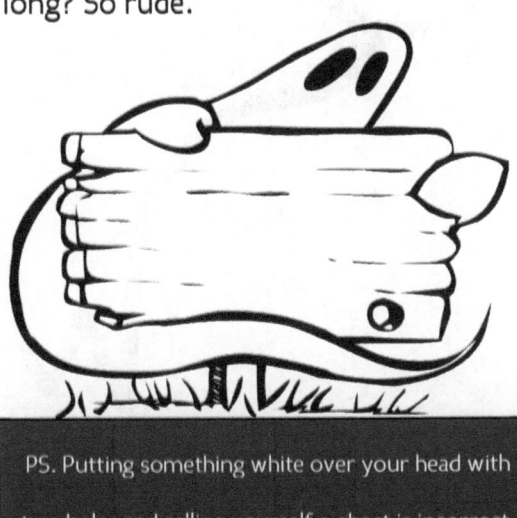

PS. Putting something white over your head with two holes and calling yourself a ghost is incorrect. If you're white with two holes, you are Laura Anne Ingraham. By the way, IngraHAM does look like a piece of ham (or like the pig on the next page).

PIGS IN A BLANKET

In my day, there were no blankets and we called them "sex offenders in 100 thread count sheets." Jeffrey Epstein would know.

Part Seven

Violence and Weapons

If you find this picture arousing, let me just remind you this is a cannon and the next part is VERY violent.

KNOCK SOMEONE OUT

What the fuck are you knocking with to make someone unconscious, a hammer? Jeffrey Dahmer tried that and now he's in jail awaiting the chair. We had a doorbell, for fuck's sake. How could he not see it? It's that thing you press that makes a sound, but what Hugh Hefner pressed also made a sound—a squirting one.

BURY THE HATCHET

Ask Carole Baskin. She knows what it means.

JUMP THE GUN

I loathe this one because, for the longest time, I thought people said, "Jump the *gum*." Have you seen a horse's *gum*? Fucking scary! Have you seen Mama June's? It's like a vagina inside out.

GUNG HO

This expression is only violent because it sounds like you're saying, "Gun, ho!"

From my personal experience, if you hear someone saying the words "gun" and "ho" in the same sentence—run for dear life!

LOOSE CANNON

Look, if there's something loose, it's not a cannon. Right, Octomom?

I hate to bring her up so often; I'm just jealous. The last time I tried sneaking in cocaine up my butt from Mexico, there was only enough room for five grams. But Octomom? I don't know the exact weight she could smuggle, because I don't know how many grams fit into a U-Haul.

"Hello, may I help you?"

"Hi, I'm calling because I'm trying to find out how many grams fit into your U-Hauls trucks."

"How many grams of what?"

"Some sort of white powder."

"Like, cocaine? You shouldn't use U-Haul for transporting cocaine, sir! It's illegal."

"So is drinking underage and driving over the limit! All I wanna do is learn how big Octomom's vagina is."

"Sir, I don't think I can help you. I think you were trying to call someone stupid, like Sarah Huckabee Sanders at 1-800-DODO."

"For real?"

"Yes, this is 1-800-UR-HOLE, an escort service in Nevada."

CUT TO THE CHASE

Are we talking about the same Chase? Chase Bank? They refused to fund me a million-dollar loan, saying I didn't have enough collateral and that my credit score had a bad grade.

First of all, not enough collateral? Girl, I'm wearing Zara and even have a savings account. I fucking *have* collateral.

Second, if my credit score has a bad grade, fine! I'll send it back to college.

Just cut to the chase and give me the damn money! I need a facelift.

SHOOT THE BREEZE

Why so violent? I don't believe in guns much like I don't believe the theorists who think we didn't land on the moon. Look, if Curiosity rover could land on Mars during intense turbulence and a fly could land on Mike Pence during the vice-presidential debates in 2020, trust me, anything is possible. So, yes. It's possible that Carole Baskin didn't kill her first husband. But she did kill a tiger who had.

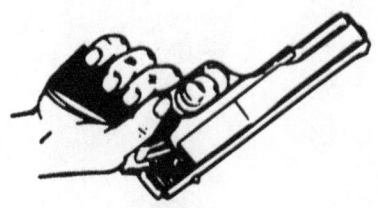

Part Eight

Body Parts

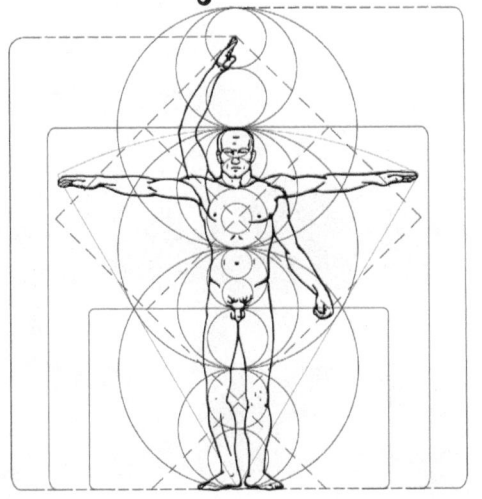

GREEN THUMB

When someone says, "My Annie has such a green thumb!" I want to vomit. Is it because Annie's an alien? No? Then why is she green, bald, and born in Roswell, New Mexico?

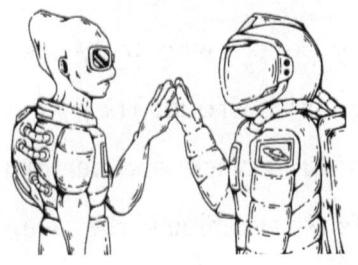

BLUE IN THE FACE

I hate this one, mainly because I've been blue in the face and blue in the balls simultaneously. The only difference is, when you talk about Jim Jarmusch from the movie *Blue in the Face*, you never know what you're looking at: his face or his crotch.

The only people who truly are blue in the face are Blue Man Group. They paint their faces blue, dress up in black, and perform on stage. The Smurfs are also blue in the face.

BTW, why are the Smurfs such perverts? They wear jizz-filled condoms on their heads and only pants. Can't they afford a shirt? They're the most famous cartoon in the world. Come on, assholes, put some clothes on. Little children are watching!

LONG IN THE TOOTH

Why is that an expression about getting old? If I'm long anywhere when I'm 95, it'll be a long list of Medicare plans: I'll have Plan A, B, C, and D.

Fun fact: this expression originated because of horses. As horses get older, their gums proportionally diminish, exposing teeth. The longer the teeth, the older the horse. I'll blow your mind: Jerry Seinfeld is 66, and I guessed it when he smiled. Now try it for yourself—smile in the mirror.

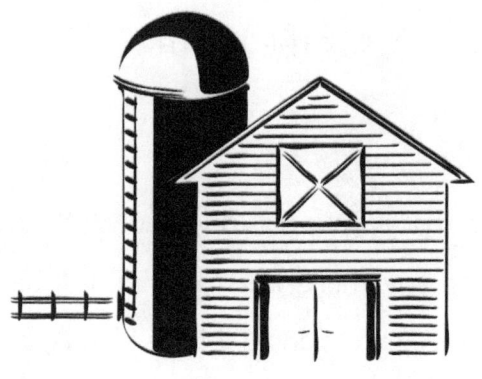

KEEP YOUR CHIN UP

What kind of pose is that? When your chin is up, that means your legs are high in the air, and I don't want to discuss your sex life. You're 78 and you enjoy getting fucked by horses. Don't give me any more visuals, please.

What I'm saying is: if your chin is up, keep it to yourself behind the closed barn door.

NO BRAINER

Why are we still talking about Lindsay Lohan? So what if she doesn't have a brain? Leave her alone! Besides, the brain is not the most essential organ. Right, Sarah Palin? The most essential organ is the gut. There are more bacteria cells in the gut than cells at the Silivry Prison Campus. The bacteria control everything right down to our mood. There's an expression: "You are what you eat," and whatever you feed the bacteria,[1] that's what you'll become. That's why I'm wondering about *The Real Housewives of Potomac*. They're such raging bitches. Do they eat dog food?

[1] Bacteria is the plural of bacterium, by the way. I'm sure you also know that cacti is the plural of cactus, and that cactus also describes Duane Chapman's cactusy face.

PLAY IT BY EAR

It's a play where you listen instead of watching. Now such plays are called podcasts, but in my day we called them the radio. Betty White, do you remember? Or, more like—guys, do you remember Betty White? She's white, her name's Betty. She's an actress.

I hate that being an actor is prestigious, but whenever *I* become dramatic, I'm suddenly a drama queen and I'm being chased out of an expensive restaurant by an angry French chef. So what if I threw a bunch of escargot snails at you? There must have been a reason! We were having a fun date and I invited you over for sex, but you told me, "We should play it by ear." WELL, NOW WHAT? Now there's an angry French chef running after me and if I wanted something French and angry, I'd move to fucking Paris!

AN ARM AND A LEG

When something costs an arm and a leg, we consider it expensive, but how does the currency conversion even work? I'm asking because I'm traveling to Vietnam with an American leg next month. Here's some pricing I pulled up from the black market/Craigslist:

Sperm = $0 (high quality; from the back alley)
Sperm = $700 (high quality; from a sperm bank)
An arm and a leg = $30
A shrew's heart = $20

So I sent a shrew's heart to Alex Kozinski. I heard he had no heart (or moral ethics), but you can't buy moral ethics or white supremacists would all have been good.

HEADS UP

Heads up: it will get dark and violent for a second and will obviously involve Carole Baskin. Did you know that after killing her husband, she took him apart and sold him by parts? That's how I ended up buying an American leg.

PS. It only cost me $5.99 plus shipping.

GIVE SOMEONE THE COLD SHOULDER

When Carole Baskin's husband died and his shoulder got cold, she gave the shoulder to a tiger. The tiger asked to warm it up, so Carole microwaved it. So stupid. She didn't cover the meat, so the tomato sauce was all over the fucking place! That's what tomato sauce does in a microwave. Yes, Carole, you're smart, but you obviously don't know shit about cooking.

TWIST SOMEONE'S ARM

Carole Baskin again.

Before sawing her husband's arm off (per H.H. Holmes' suggestion), she tried to twist it off, which is the dumbest thing ever. Why? Because of Carole, we had to add "twist someone's arm" into the dictionary. My Merriam-Webster is already 1000 pages long and if we keep adding more expressions, millions of trees will die.

Carole, I beg of you! Stop killing your husbands! The forest is thinning.

Part Nine

Numbers

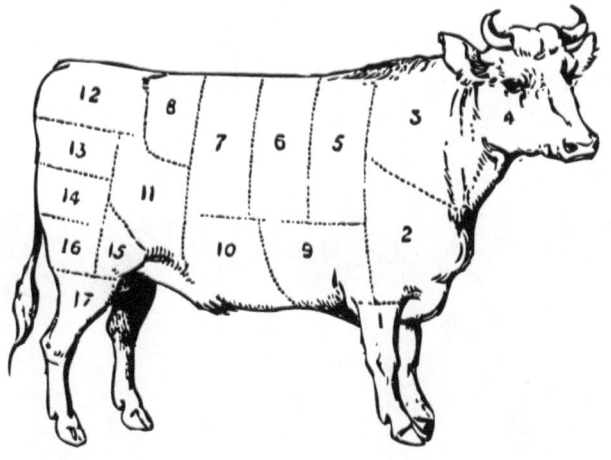

FIVE O'CLOCK SHADOW

When some people shave at seven in the morning, they get a shadow by five that night—a five o'clock shadow—and not a minute later. Boom! A shadow at five o'clock! Do they have some impressive growth hormones, or are they taking biotin?

A five o'clock shadow is a telltale sign of who's gay in your office. If they have a five o'clock shadow, you know they swallowed lots of semen during lunch, as semen has a ton of biotin. It's a no brainer then that Madonna shows up with a mustache under her nose too.

ZERO

TOLERANCE

Zero tolerance is when no rule violation will be tolerated—period! That's a little bit regime-ey, doncha think? Just because there was a sign saying, NO SMOKING ALLOWED, that's no reason to punish me. It was so smoky, I didn't even see the fucking sign.

I think we're allowed to make mistakes. The more mistakes you make early on, the better. You can't really punish a two-year-old for burying his cat or an eight-year-old for drowning a sibling, but when you're eleven—like in Mary Bell's case—and you still kill, then something *is* wrong with you.

In 1968, at the age of ten or eleven, Mary Bell strangled a three- and a four-year-old in Newcastle upon Tyne in the United Kingdom. Her prostitute mother—Betty McCrickett—was so pissed off and embarrassed about it that she tried giving little Mary some sleeping pills to kill her off. The mother wanted to make it look like an accident. Mary Bell was smarter, however, and didn't take the pills.

On December 17, 1968, the judge decided that sweet Mary was a "very grave risk to other children." Yeah, no shit! He sentenced her to twelve years in prison.

You know what? If the mother, Betty McCrickett, allowed Mary to drown a few kittens early on, Mary would've had it out of her system by eleven, and two children would've been saved, doncha think? Look, I'm not suggesting anything; I'm just *saying*. But if you have a child, please watch them closely from two to about nine. If they say things like, "Mommy, do all people go to heaven?" or "Daddy, will Jimmy feel pain if I stab him with our chef's knife?" take a little action! Take them hunting or fishing, or to a Taco Bell.

Last time, after a Taco Bell, I had such severe diarrhea, I spent hours in the john—with no time left to kill anyone.

Allow your children to be expressive with crayons. If they use too much red, take them to the zoo and say, "Just because that monkey resembles your daddy, it doesn't mean anything. It's just a coincidence. You'll learn later about incest in our family or why you're so slow and not on the up and up."

If nothing works, you can always offer them up for adoption. Talk to your neighbors. Is there a family in your community with too many children whose parents may wanna get rid of? Send your stabby Mary or kicky Johnny there!

Last thing you could do is move to a busy city like New York or Los Angeles. Violence mostly happens in rural communities where people murder just to feel like they've been productive and accomplished something that day. I've lived in New York for ten years, but it only feels like a day because I'm fucking busy. On most days I'm so busy I even forget to be nice.

So what did we learn today, cool cats and kittens? Practice tolerance, make mistakes, and try—just try—to avoid burying your husbands. #amirite?

Creepy Mary Bell, circa 1969.

BEHIND THE EIGHT BALL

Why is it that when you're behind the eight ball, you're at a disadvantage? It's just a warm-up. The fun starts when more people show up.

These days sex is so taboo, but apparently, back in the day, movie stars had wild sex parties. For instance, Tallulah Bankhead was not only behind an eighth ball, but also behind a sixth clitoris.

Forget Tallulah Bankhead. Winston Blackmore, the leader of the Mormon fundamentalist sect, had 24 wives and over 145 children. That's the spirit! Stamina. Dedication.

There was so much semen in the house that when the cleaning lady showed up, she got glued to the floor and became wife #25.

PLEAD THE FIFTH

I love, love, loooove this one. I went on a shopping spree at a weed dispensary in Denver, Colorado, and when I got home my ex-boyfriend confronted me with, "How much money did you spend this time?"

I said, "I plead the fifth."

"Whose dead body is it in the corner?"

"I plead the fifth!"

"You're not in the court of law!"

"I know, bitch! I'm so high I'm on cloud nine!"

CLOUD NINE

When you're on cloud nine, that means you're happy and in a state of bliss—like when you orgasm or when another sex offender gets arrested. I was elated when in 2004, Paul Reubens (who played Pee-wee Herman) registered as a sex offender for possession of images of minors having sex, and then elated again in 2015 when a former Subway spokesman Jared Fogle was sentenced to fifteen years in prison for child porn. People must be held accountable!

What I don't understand is how child porn is even made. How are those children filming porn? For example, when I was a child I couldn't afford a Coke, let alone lights, cameras, and clean sheets. As a child, the only time I heard "Action!" was when my mom gave me three seconds to fall asleep, and the only time "stroking" was involved was when my uncle had a stroke and had to be rushed to the hospital.[1]

[1] I've just realized this is getting sinister real fast. So let me finish by saying: have sex when you're eighteen, and for fuck's sake ask for consent. Then you'll both be on cloud nine.

86ED

Have you ever been 86ed from a bar? Well, apparently John Barrymore did in the 1920s. He had a drinking problem and that's how that expression originated.

Boring!

Nothing is duller than a drinking celebrity, not even the three cells in Sarah Palin's brain.

Drinking, eating, or breathing are not problems but a part of our biology. Have you been to sixth grade? Biology is in the curriculum.

Another annoying number is 27. When you

die at 27, you become a member of a special club. Oh, really? I don't fucking think so.

Look, Mickey Mouse Club was a club, and it was frequented by talentless children who wanted to become famous and what they got was drug problems instead. Sweet!

Another real club is Lester's Gentlemen's Club on 42nd Street, where unemployed bombshells go to have sushi served off their tits.

So back to my point. The last time I checked, Brian Jones and Amy Winehouse, weren't in any of these clubs. They were decomposing in a cemetery in England.[1]

[1] Why is En*gland* a *gland* and not, for example, En*organ* or En*cyst*?[2]

[2] Encyst is the British spelling of incest.[3]

[3] If you really want to know my opinion, I believe there's some sort of incest going on with the Palins. Sarah Palin brought us Trig, Track, Bristol, Willow, and Piper, and what did Bristol bring us? Sailor Grace, Atlee Bay, and Tripp Easton Mitchell Johnson[4] and they were all slow children. Sailor Grace thought she was a sailor, so she cursed like one, and Atlee Bay thought she was a bay, and that's where Sailor parked her boats.

[4] Yes, Tripp Easton Mitchell Johnson is one person. Before he was born, a moose smacked Bristol Palin on the head and she became even stupider—if you can believe that—so she couldn't come up with a single name for her baby. She just threw a book of baby names at the clerk from the bureau of vital records, and the clerk picked four at random.

A DIME A DOZEN

If you want good Chinese food you go to Chinatown, if you want false news you watch Fox News, and if you need to solve a murder you turn to Judy Buenoano.

The "Black Widow" poisoned her husband with arsenic, drowned her son, and tried killing her fiancé with a car bomb. The most annoying thing about the "Black Widow" is that she wasn't even black. That's racist, in my opinion, to always blame black people for everything.

Anyhow, her motive was the insurance money: $240,000. Money is always the motive, and the significant other is always the one who kills. Judy Buenoano's story is a dime a dozen and the bitch is from Florida, so, like, how could you not see it coming?

PUT TWO AND TWO TOGETHER

I hate this expression because I'm an English major and I hate math, but I put some twos and twos together for you, so you don't have to. You're welcome.

1. Sam Smith + weight loss = liposuction
2. Adele + weight loss = Katy Perry
3. Lack of moral code + tax avoidance = Donald Trump
4. D.B. Cooper + his money = Amazon startup circa 1994
5. Aliens + sand = Egyptian pyramids

And the last one you can do yourself:

6. Big cats + missing husband = ?

Part Ten

Money and Names

BREAK A BILL

When I worked at Dunkin', I hated it when people asked me to break a twenty-dollar-bill. You're exchanging money for the same amount just in smaller denominations. What's the fucking point? You're not getting any more money this way. If you're going to watch a drag show, then don't go to Dunkin', you needy whore. Go to the bank.

Before Dunkin', I worked for a mafia guy, and "breaking a bill" meant something very different.

BIGGER BANG FOR YOUR BUCK

More money could buy you a bigger prostitute in the good old days, and you called her (or him) a "bigger bang for your buck."

When you go to the Louvre, stop by the Mona Lisa. What do you see? Don't you think the painting is too small—much smaller than you expected? Back then, art supplies (and big, doughy models) were expensive, so the poplar wood panel for the Mona Lisa painting was nothing but a quick trip to the woods. Mona Lisa herself was a short, tiny person, and that's because Leonardo da Vinci couldn't afford anyone bigger on five francs, which is a shame. After all, with just two more franks, we could have had someone larger at the Louvre. Anyone from Denise Borino to Val Kilmer.

I hate Mona Lisa. The bitch had such an important job to become the most recognized face in history, and what is she wearing? Did she come to pose straight from a walk of shame? Why couldn't she, for example, wear something smart casual? Absurd! If I wanted to look at a slut, I'd watch *Pretty Woman*.

Yo, is this Mona Lisa or Putin with a wig?

PETER OUT

I hate this expression because of Peter Paul Rubens. His first name is a fucking verb (to peter out) and his last name is a sandwich (Reuben). How much needier and narcissistic could you get?

I loathe other needy names/verbs: Flip, Pierce, Mark, Pat, Skip, and Sue. I can tolerate Drew because it's in the past tense, and I kind of forgive Dawn and Rose because they are nouns (and nouns don't count).

The name I loathe the most is Owen. I'm not Owen you anything, fucker! So go and Sue someone else.

Besides, "Peter"—if you say it to someone who's Russian—would sound like a bad word describing a homosexual man, the same as the word "f****t."

No, not "fat," "florist," or "flamboyant"—but precisely the word you're thinking. It starts with the British word for a cigarette. Fag.

I hate that word! I also hate the word florist.

A florist is someone who can put a few flowers in a vase. I do this all the time, but I don't call myself a florist. How is that a profession? It's like saying you're a bus operator whenever you take the bus or like saying you're gay just because you've been pegged a few times.

I think we should relax. Fine, if you wanna call yourself a florist because you could tie a dozen roses together, then call yourself a florist. The last time when Ted Bundy tied something together, nobody called him a florist; they called him an electric chair. AND WHAT A SHAME! He fucking perfected the butterfly loop knot.

JOHN HANCOCK

I loathe this one because of my accountant Steve. Steve is very annoying and talks nonstop, so he was talking and I wasn't listening. Then I heard he said, "Give me your—BLAH, BLAH, BLAH—cock," so I started listening.

"Are you sure, Steve?" *Should I give him my cock?* I thought.

"Yeah," he said, "give it to me, boy!"

I unzipped my pants, pulled out my schlong, and we're no longer friends. Why couldn't he just ask for a signature like a normal person? In the end, I got myself a new accountant who's Polish and who doesn't use stupid American expressions!

By the way, John Hancock means a signature and is named after John Hancock, who served as president of the Second Continental Congress.

He signed a document BY ACCIDENT and today we call any signature after him. That's bullshit!

Like, why did nobody call nonstop diarrhea after me? You come to a doctor and he tells you, "Oh, fuck! You've got Taylor's. Eat more fiber and avoid public pools."

Besides, I hate when things happen by accident, especially when it comes to pregnancies. How are they EVER accidental? Put two and two together, people! A penis and a vagina met, so what else did you expect if not a baby? An 11-inch mattress?

There's a legend that a Chinese cook invented fireworks 2000 years ago. He mixed charcoal, sulfur, and saltpeter and compressed them into a bamboo tube. What the FUCK was he cooking? I understand that cast iron pans cost a lot of money, but it's either cast iron or castrated by fireworks. Your choice.

Part Eleven

Travel

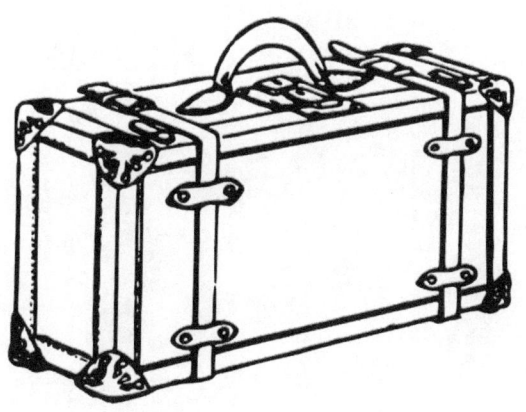

UP ONE'S ALLEY

Last time I checked, the only thing inside an alley was a black homeless cat, and then Carole Baskin killed it and buried it, and a black locust tree grew in its place. If you don't know what I'm talking about, go back and read PART THREE: PUT LIPSTICK ON A PIG. Did you know that a black locust is a hardwood tree? The only hardwood Carole Baskin had ever received was at a baseball game and Luke Voit hit her with a baseball bat. (Yes, that's how she got fucked up.)

CLIMB ON THE BANDWAGON

I hate it when people start climbing things. That means they're usually up to no good.

In 2016, a man named Stephen Rogata climbed Trump World Tower using suction cups. I was outraged because that day I had my suction cup therapy, and the fucker had stolen my suction cups. The masseuse ended up sucking my back with his mouth, and he has these huge horse teeth (he was a redneck from Alabama) and I was hurt and bleeding for a week.

I once dated a firefighter who had to leave in the middle of a blowjob to rescue a pussycat that climbed a tree and couldn't come down. Ugh, the pussycat was so stupid. People, always have a back-up plan! Like, I always bring a bottle of vodka whenever I take an elevator. Why? In case I get stuck and get bored. Whenever I climb

trees, I always make sure they're cut, sanded, and shaped like a bench.

Stephen Rogata, you fucking asshole, if you must climb something in the future, climb Mount Everest. Chances are (99%) you'll die and no suction cups are needed—and I can't bear another suction-less massage.

PS. What was the tallest mountain before Mount Everest was discovered? The answer is Mount Everest, Dumb Dumb. Here's another one that will occupy you for a day or two: How do you spell "cat"?

UNDER THE BUS

First of all, what the fuck are you doing under the bus? Second of all, is it the M60 or the M16? There's an enormous difference. I have a flight from LaGuardia Airport and the M60 is fifty minutes late. If you have a fetish to be under things, crawl under a man and get fucked somewhere other than your head, you moron.

Did you know that New York City buses live for only 12 to 15 years (like a cat)? The buses are then shredded and sent for scraps (or drowned in the ocean), which what happens to Carole Baskin's cats and husbands as well.

Why does a bus—metal and all—only live from 12 to 15 years? Even Robocop lived longer. Look, if I'm feeling unwell, I take a few ibuprofens and I'm fine. Change a tire and get rid of the urine-stained seats. Problem solved. The bus is good as new.

Look, I simply HATE littering. Exchanging thousands of buses every 12 to 15 years is a lot of iron, glass, and plastic, and that pollutes our oceans. Last time I took a swim at Sandy Hook Beach (the nude one; Parking Lot G; you're welcome!), I cut my toe on a glass window and got an infection—and I'm not insured. How will I pay for my hospital visit if the Republicans keep pushing to abolish Obamacare?

If you wanna throw us under the bus or throw buses into the Atlantic ocean—fine. First, fix the health crisis. Thanks.

To the lazy asshole who drew this: when you draw a white square and two circles, that's not a bus. That's Emily Deschanel's face.

RIDE SHOTGUN

I find it incredibly rude that New York City cab drivers don't let anyone ride shotgun. You always have to sit in the back. I get carsick back there. Why is the driver surprised that I didn't tip him and threw up on the Plexiglass?

GOING DOWN MEMORY LANE

If you need to go down on something, choose a penis or a burger, whichever is bigger. Make sure the burger is at least a quarter pounder and the penis is at least 6" or otherwise, why even bother? #amirite?

BLAST FROM THE PAST

This expression is from astronomy. If you don't know what astronomy is, skip to the next expression.

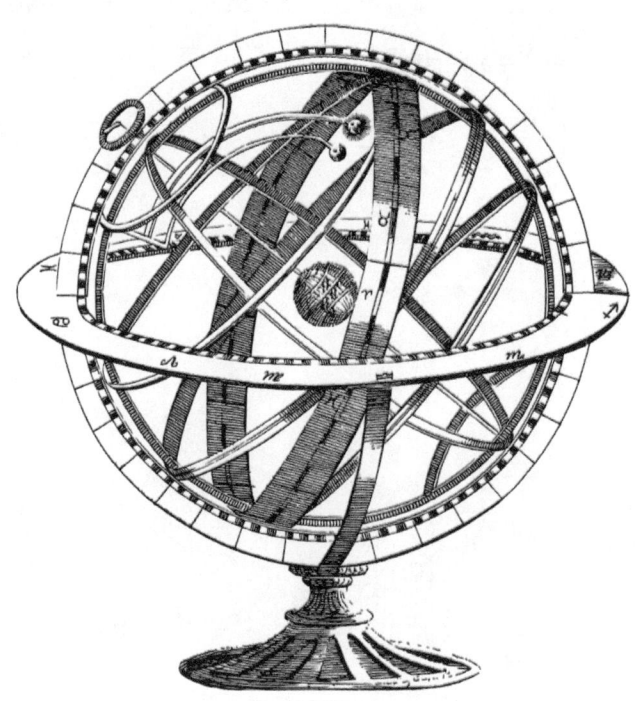

The Big Bang happened thirteen billion years ago. No, the Big Bang is not slang for an "orgy."

The Big Bang is when there was nothing in the universe, then BAM—everything exploded like a motherfucker. You, me, and the toilet in which you're sitting reading this book are made from the same material. Then why, you're wondering, are the Palins, the Trumps, and the Bushes so different from the rest of us? What kind of an explosion made that happened, right?

Fret no more and I'll tell you: there was an explosion at a shit-processing plant in Poughkeepsie, New York.

IT'S ALL DOWNHILL FROM HERE

No shit! Now in my thirties, I wake up and my face is twice bigger from water retention. There's no more morning wood. In fact, it's no longer a forest but a valley. You have one beer and you're hungover for a week.

However, there's a silver lining: I can afford my own apartment, my clothes no longer have holes in them, and I've learned how to make my bed, fold laundry, and give head without accidents. Let's just say a Prince Albert can indeed get stuck on a tongue ring.

That's evolution: from a wild party beast on drugs to a housewife who Marie-Kondos the shit out of every drawer. No more tongue ring, either. Just a nice, long, moist blowjob.

SCOOT OVER

The couch is so roomy, but you still need me to move, you lazy asshole? That's fine, but buy me a fucking scooter first.

Actually, that's not why I hate this expression. I'm a stickler for purity and "to scoot" means "to slide," and the last time I checked, I was not a fucking snake. For example, I don't swallow things whole like a snake. I have the decency to chew.

You know who swallows *a lot?* Condoleezza Rice. That's why she doesn't have any children. Come on, Condoleezza! We need more Rice in the world.

Actually, I hate rice. It's white, boring, and doesn't add anything to the table regarding nutrition.

Besides, rice is everywhere and I hate stuff that's off-trend. Right now, it's all about farro, quinoa, and hemp. They're different, colorful, and healthy, so they're basically queer, and if I want "regular," I'll invite my straight neighbor Jason. He also is white, boring, and doesn't add anything to the table.

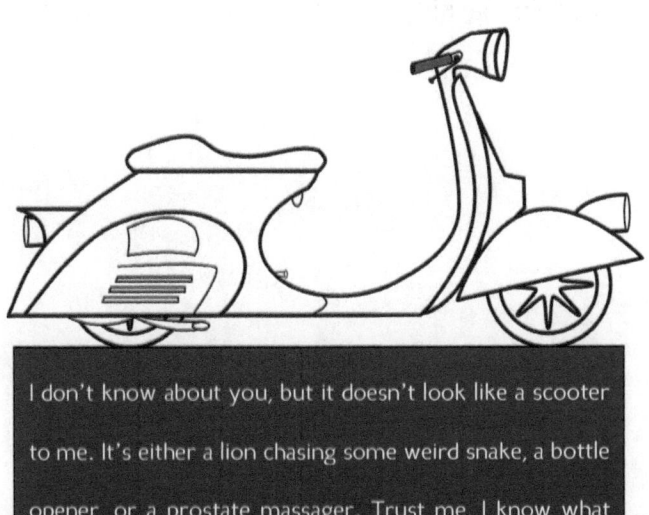

I don't know about you, but it doesn't look like a scooter to me. It's either a lion chasing some weird snake, a bottle opener, or a prostate massager. Trust me, I know what one looks like. Because I'm not a prude.

GO DUTCH

It means to split down the middle. In my day, we didn't call it "going Dutch." We called it "pulling a Carole Baskin." Hiyah—with a hatchet—straight down the middle!

That's right, bitches. No more fun for you.

This is it.

THE END

Note

This is not a coloring book, but you bought it so do whatever you want with it. There's purposefully a lot of white space, but not just so you could write down recipes and phone numbers. White space is soothing, and the absence of text draws your eyes to the text.

That's a technique.

See what I did there?

Please do not take anything in this book seriously, for it was written as a comedic tome, similar to *War and Peace* and *To Kill a Mockingbird*. And last, do not give this book to kids under the age of seven. Simply because I don't trust youngsters. They would rip it apart, and I hate it when my work is disrespected.

Acknowledgment

The author wishes to thank the following people: Andres, Mary, Jess, and Gian for editorial work, words of encouragement, and feedback. Thank you Tanja for the book cover design, thank you Marilyn for the images, and thank you Jessica for the interior design.

About the Author

Jeremy Taylor performed his first standup on a bus in Kazakhstan at the age of nine, which he writes about in his memoir. Since then, he wrote and performed comedy spasmodically.

In college, he scripted and starred in *KVN*,[1] an abbreviation for "the club of funny and witty people," which consists of standup, musical, sketch, and improv elements—and is a national competition akin to NBC's *Last Comic Standing*.

After immigrating to the United States from Russia, Jeremy performed standup in New York City.

Books that make him laugh are *I Hate Everyone Starting with Me* by Joan Rivers, *My Horizontal Life: A Collection of One-Night Stands* by Chelsea Handler, *Are You There God? It's Me, Margaret* by Judy Blume, and *R Is for Ricochet* by Sue Grafton.

His favorite TV shows are *I Love Lucy, Crazy Ex-Girlfriend, Kim's Convenience, Schitt's Creek, Friends,*

Sex and the City, Broad City, Emily in Paris, It's Always Sunny in Philadelphia, The Good Place, Saturday Night Life, Young & Hungry, Never Have I Ever, and *Moesha*.

Books by Jeremy Taylor: *Diary of a Mad Gay Man;* a novel, *The Cornerstones of Happiness*; and a memoir, *Noodles with Grandma: And Other Stories from Our Homestead in Kazakhstan*

Instagram: jeremy.taylor.ny
Twitter: jeremytaylor_ny

[1] "*KVN* . . . is a Soviet and then Russian humour [sic] TV show and an international competition where teams (usually college students) compete by giving funny answers to questions and showing prepared sketches, that originated in the Soviet Union. . . ." Source: Wikipedia.

www.ingramcontent.com/pod-product-compliance
Lightning Source LLC
Chambersburg PA
CBHW021951160426
43209CB00001B/2